my father's eyes my mother's rage

my father's eyes, my mother's rage
ISBN: 978-1-7381510-0-4

trigger warning:

this book contains themes of childhood trauma, domestic violence, depression and suicide, which may be distressing for some readers. please read with care and seek support if needed.

for my mother,

who taught me everything that
love should and shouldn't be.

wherever you are,
I hope you've found peace.

(and I hope that you are proud of me)

roots of pain 9

dangerous love – 79

invisible wounds – 145

no more tomorrow – 167

the renewal – 191

nurturing – 237

my father's eyes, my mother's rage

1. roots of pain

mother and father wound

damn right I'm angry.

I've spent my life recovering from things
that I should have been protected from.

I was too young to become a ghost full of grief,
children are supposed to be happy and free.

don't tell me I wouldn't be who I am today,
without all the struggles I faced.

I already know that. I could have been a kid
instead of being forced to grow up.

the people who were supposed to protect me,
failed me. no amount of healing will change that.

damn right I'm angry,
I'll never get my childhood back.

I have my father’s eyes,

and every time I look at myself,
I see him walking away.

if he had stayed,
I think I would’ve been okay.

but I keep searching for him in men
that will never love me the way I need.

I needed my father to love me;
I wish he didn’t leave.

as a young child, I was already exhausted.
my mother told anyone who would listen
not to be fooled by my sweet face;
I was hell and caused too much trouble.
was it too much to want to be loved
as all children deserve to be loved?

I was begging for love, angry to be seen.
exhaustion grew inside of me,
as she introduced me as a burden
more than she said my name.

instead of holding me safe, she pushed me away
and quieted my voice by making me ashamed.
she screamed until my identity became fatigue.
I had so much to say but it was easier to sleep.

then when I cried about things I couldn't achieve,
she told me it was my fault and called me lazy.

the first time I felt unsafe,
was when my father walked away.

my mother begged him to stay,
but he left so quietly, with nothing to say.

that's when my mother gave birth to rage;
she poured it inside of me,

when my father walked away.

I am a mother to my mother,
and I never wanted to be.

it just fell into place
when she fell to her knees.

I was a child, afraid inside,
telling her that everything would be alright.

raising myself while raising my mother,
but all I ever wanted, was to be her daughter.

refugee in my own home,
fleeing my mother's attack,
in my room alone.

I’m too young to wish for death,
but I can't take much more than this.

when will she realize I’m not the enemy?
she swears to god that she shouldn’t of had me.

insults shoot from her mouth like bullets;
I really wish there was no war between us.

the little girl in the purple room
sits on the edge of her bed,
listening to the sound of footsteps
to see if she's upset.

the little girl in the purple room
prays for her dad to come back,
because if he does, her mom won't be sad.

the little girl in the purple room
gets yelled at a lot; her mom
slams the door until it breaks off.

the little girl in the purple room
wishes things would change,
but no matter what she does
it always stays the same.

the little girl in the purple room
doesn't want to exist, so she
locks herself inside the room,
and hopes for it all to end.

my mother said she shouldn't have
been a mother, but I think she meant,
she shouldn't have had a daughter.

I can still hear her voice inside my head,
regretting me incessantly.

and I can still feel my heart inside my chest,
breaking endlessly.

everything was my fault,
I could never do anything right.
she cut herself open, my existence was the knife.

my mother wanted me to heal her,
to be the salt in her wound,
but I was also suffering and needed healing too.

she blamed me religiously
and destroyed everything in her path.
if I didn't comply, I would feel her wrath.

my birth was an annoyance, a burden,
one more thing she didn't need.
there was no solution to her misery,
when her misery was me.

I grew up in a family where my parent's emotions,
or lack of, was more important than my own.

since I was very young, I went through my emotions
alone. what I needed and how I felt stayed inside,
until it became too much, and I raged and cried.

I was desperate for my feelings to be acknowledged,
not ignored. now I have a bad habit of holding
it all in until I explode.

when your mother is your first love,
you can search to the ends of the earth
and never find any love comparable.

when your mother is your first heartbreak,
no love will ever fill the void
of feeling so unloved by her.

she loves to scream at me when I am weak;
my helplessness makes her angry.

I am just a foolish girl
and that's all I'll ever be.

I want compassion from my mother,
but she can't be compassionate with me.

still, *I love her, I love her, I love her.*
after all, she is my mother.

when I was a child and I said,
"I can't! I'm not good enough!"

I needed someone wiser and kinder to tell me,
"you can and you are!"

how different things could have been
if I had heard those words.

if someone had believed in me
more than I believed in myself.

I never believed in ghosts,
until my father walked out
of my life and became one.

I wasn't afraid of monsters under
my bed, my fear was making my
mother upset.

it's confusing to be a child and
feel scared of those who should
be comforting you.

to live in a home filled with sorrow
and anger, haunted by the very ones
who say there is nothing to be afraid of.

they say a girl needs her father,
but my father didn't need me.

he preferred his idea of life,
over the one that god gave him.

I don't blame him though;
he felt trapped and he couldn't grow
because of my mother's need for control.

she tried to love and didn't know how,
but he is the one who left me as a child.

it's true what they say, I did need my father,
but my father didn't need a daughter.

she pushed everyone else away,
but my empathy forced me to stay.

her words are getting to me though.
I can't stand her tone, the rasp in her throat.

I don't know if I can take any more.
I want her to change, but *I know that she won't.*

the lonely child is loud
because she is never listened to.

she is out of control,
because it's the only way to get attention.

the lonely child only ever wanted acceptance and
love; being quiet made her unnoticeable and untouched.

so, she settled for chaos and anger,
because any attention was better than none.

my mother didn't want to hurt me,
but she was broken.
her brokenness cut into me
and made me bleed.

she didn't know how to love,
or at least how to love me.
it didn't even matter that she hurt me;
I just wanted her to be sorry.

she said that she loved me,
but it often felt like hate.
when I finally had enough and tried to be free,
she looked at me with desperation and cried,

"you are abandoning me!"

so, I stayed and I suffered,
and I did my best to love her.
as a woman, I have so much empathy
for my mother, but *as a daughter, I have so much anger.*

my friends think my mom is nice and she is,
(sort of), especially when they're around.

she is as nice as she can be,
she can hold her anger while others are there.

I have her ability to pretend everything is fine
while falling apart inside.

she taught me that honesty wasn't loyalty,
and it was better to lie about what was happening.

so, I keep smiling and hiding and hoping it will
all work out in the end, but it's getting harder
to pretend.

when my friends ask me if everything’s okay,
I tell them nothing is the matter.

we are not so different than each other,
in the end, I am my mother's daughter.

I am jealous of the mothers and daughters
who are each other's everything.
I love my mom so much
but she treats me like the enemy.

I wanted a mother to braid my hair
and say that I was beautiful.
I wanted to share clothes and secrets,
without being scared she would explode.

I wanted her gentle guidance and kindness;
I needed to feel safe and at peace.
I wanted the kind of mother-daughter
relationship that didn't break me.

when my father decided to leave,
my mother gave him a million reasons to stay.

out of all the reasons to stay,
I thought he would consider one,
but I have never been enough.

I imagine a world
where I am good enough for my mother.

a world where compliments were given over
criticism and making mistakes was okay.

I imagine a world where just being myself
didn't disappoint her and no matter my failures
she was proud of me.

a world where she was as kind to me behind
closed doors as she was when people were watching.

I imagine a world where I don't have to heal
from the pain caused by my mother.

a world where I was protected from trauma,
not fed it fresh from the womb.

I imagine a world
where my mother wasn't my wound.

when I was a little girl,
I watched in awe of those
who had confidence in themselves.

they knew how to dress,
their favourite colour,
and favourite song.

I never had time to discover myself;
I was always too busy worrying
about going home.

it was so hard to admit that my father would
never be able to love me the way he should.

I must stop believing I can't be loved,
just because he couldn't.

who was my mother, before she was my mother?
before my father left and devastated every ounce
of her being, who was she?

who was my mother before she contorted herself
to be exactly what he wanted her to be and still
not be enough?

who was she before all the sadness and anger?
was she happy and at peace?
who was my mother before she had me?

my childhood home,
the first place I felt alone.

the first place I felt my mother's love
and my mother's rage, our family home
where my father walked away.

after he left, she was never the same;
she begged for forgiveness,
but he said it was too late.

the walls watched my mother
become nothing but bones,
and heard me crying for hours
at night on my own.

I am envious of those who had
a happy place to grow. the first place
I ever felt alone, was my childhood home.

I try to speak my truth, but I cry.

when I would express my opinion,
my mother saw it as a chance to fight.

my father never sat with me in sadness;
he would get up and say goodbye.

so, when I feel emotion,
it's hard to express what's inside.

now that I am older,
I understand the reasons why,
but I still cannot speak my truth
without having to cry.

dear mom,

I know you were hurt and betrayed,
but why did you hurt me the same?
I was just a little girl and didn't know
anything except that your anger never changed.

I needed you to guide me softly,
not judge me harshly. if I had been held
instead of hit, I know it all would have been different.

am I supposed to be grateful to have survived
one trauma after the other? they all could have
been avoided if I'd had a healthy mother.

I hate myself for loving you so deeply;
look at all the pain you gave me.
you shouldn't hurt the ones you love;
I was a child and I needed to be taken care of.

how many times do I need to forgive you
before I am guilty of breaking my own heart?
I owed you my life, so you took my childhood
before it had time to start.

I ache for my father’s love,
although he couldn't give me very much.
when he did, it was always enough.

it would sustain me, it would fill me up,
I just needed a little bit of his love.

that's how I learned to survive on crumbs.

she told me I would understand,
when I grew up and had a daughter.

a daughter just like me;
disobedient, angry, and unruly.

she made me hate myself,
more than anything else.

I believed everything she told me,
as if her words were holy.

to this day, *I pray I don't have a daughter*.
that way, there is never a chance
to end up like my mother.

I have my mother's rage,
and my father's ability to walk away.

this, I've learned,
is *a very lonely combination.*

home was supposed to be the place I felt safe,
but it was always on fire and I was locked inside
with no escape.

I didn't know that home could be any different
than the hell I lived in. my mom said it was my fault,
I always pushed her to the limit.

I was an innocent child, with no bad intentions.
I just wanted to be loved and protected.

I wonder what kind of
woman I would have been,

if my father had stayed and my mother
hadn't disintegrated before my eyes.

if my life had been enough reason for them,
I wonder who I'd be.

forgiving my father,
although he isn't sorry.

my forgiveness is my weakness;
I always accept apologies I never receive,
but I wish he was sorry or at least pretended to be.

why were all the other women
more important to him than his daughter?
they must've had so much more to offer.

he is a man and that doesn't stop
just because he has a daughter.
what good is a woman that he can't touch?
I wasn't enough and always too much.

he never asked for my forgiveness,
but I forgive him. I cannot hold on to this resentment.

after all, even present fathers are absent.

they ask me why I can't sleep;
I haven't slept properly since I was sixteen.

since I woke up with new eyes
after I thought I’d cried myself to death,
hugging the pillow and gasping for breath.

wishing my mother had been a mother,
although now I know she did her best.

years later with the same eyes,
in a different bed, I wonder how
I ended up like this.

hugging the pillow and gasping for breath,
I’m trying not to cry myself to death.

I imagine my father as a child,
the youngest of four, a happy little boy.

he thought he was strong,
until he wasn't strong enough.

"get up! boys don't cry,
don't let me see a tear in your eye!"

his father was a man's man, and he was his only son.
he wouldn't let him be anything he didn't want.

when his father became unhappy, he went
searching for contentment in another family.

his mother was numb to emotion,
soft and sweet but terribly broken.

when I imagine this,
it's so easy to see what's coming.

he had to feel the pain or keep on running.

(he kept on running)

my mother didn't deserve
what she went through,
but neither did I.

I remember praying for her happiness
because if she was happy,
it would all be fine.

she was anger and sadness and terror.
she let the darkness
overtake her.

I don't want to be like my mother.
I want to be happy before I die.

my mother didn't deserve
what she went through,
but neither did I.

I guess my father is a good guy.

he is as good as he can be
and he loves within his own capacity.

he is funny and I have his sense of humor.
that's why I laugh as I walk away from pain,
just like him.

he taught me a lot by not teaching me at all,
except to run when things get hard.

so, I keep running into the next man's arms,
hoping he will hold me tighter than the last,
but it never lasts.

(and I learned it all from my dad)

searching for love in all the wrong places,
thrilled by the chase, until I hate it.

we are not so different than each other.
when all is said and done,

I am my father's daughter.

the difference between my mother and father:

my mother was loyal in hurting me and loving me.
no matter how bad it got,
she always stayed.

my father was loyal in hurting me and leaving me.
no matter how good it was,
he never stayed.

in the book of my life, there are pages left bare,
the love between a father and daughter
should have been there.

he was a shadow, a void unseen,
there will always be an emptiness
where he could have been.

my eyes have been searching for his love,
for his presence to fill up some space.
now it’s been so long without him,
I recognize his absence more than his face.

I'm not the apple of their eye,
but the thorn in their side.

they love me out of obligation,
I am their mistaken creation.

they love me because they have no other choice.
my life is a burden they can't avoid.

obviously, my parents love me,
parents are obliged to love their children.

but I know in their heart,
they wish that I was different.

once on my birthday, my dad bought me the
most beautiful ring. the stone was blue quartz,
it was the colour of his eyes.

I wore it every day; I cherished it. I was always
aware of it on my finger, making sure I could
feel it hugging me, to ensure it didn't get lost.

one day, I suddenly noticed its absence. I looked
down at my finger and it was gone. how could
I lose the ring when I never took it off?

I searched for it everywhere, without it I didn't
recognize my hand. it was a reminder of how
quickly something you love can be gone,
just like my dad.

I wouldn't exist without them,
that is their power over me.
it is why I cannot understand my existence.

if I was not wanted by the ones
who should love me the most,
why am I here?

she was so sweet without the anger,
innocent like a baby.

she would say I was so wise
and then ask for my advice, *she trusted me.*

I couldn't abandon her,
even when her cruelty outweighed her humanity.

some days I think that nobody in the world
has ever loved their mother more than me.

I am half of my father and half of my mother.
the best and worst of them exist in me together.

my father can’t look at me
without getting up to leave,

and my mother stares into my eyes
for hours because he is all she can see.

dear dad,

I remember when I thought you could do no wrong;
now I realize all the wrong things you've done,
but I would instantly accept your apology
if you were man enough to give me one.

I needed the kind of dad who would intimidate
every stupid boy who wanted to date me,
look them in the eye and make them afraid
to break me.

when I was in a puddle of tears
from feeling not enough,
I needed a dad to pick me back up.
I needed your guidance, your presence, your love,
and I swear if you took one step toward me,
I would run into your arms.

but you keep walking away,
and I'm too tired for the chase.
so I sit with the sadness
because it's the only thing that stays.

my mother gave her life and sanity
for my father and our family.

she showed me what happens when you
turn your back on yourself for everyone else.

I learned that love doesn't conquer all,
and there is no prince to catch my fall.

she abandoned herself and called it sacrifice,
then she died unhappy, pretending it was a good life.

who am I without a war?

war is my mother.
war is my father.
war taught me how to love.

I want to stop fighting,
but war is who I've become.

when I became a mother,
I could no longer turn away from the pain.

how could my parents do that to me?
how could my mother have thought it was okay?
how could my father so easily turn away?

I would do anything to protect my child
from emotional and physical pain.

why didn't my parents feel the same?

a kitchen table with four chairs,
three empty. he eats alone.

he thought the woman he
left us for would be the one,
but he attracts women just like him:
they leave as fast as they come.

he didn't want to be married or to be a dad.
now he’s alone in an empty house,
feeling the sadness of being left.

my mother said she wished she could hold me,
and that it would take away my pain.

I wanted to go back in time,
hold her as a child and do the same.

maybe then she wouldn't have
made all those mistakes.

but we cannot become healers
without acceptance of our own brokenness.

so now that she's gone,
I'm learning to love myself
enough for both of us.

I couldn't even cry the day
I realized my dad would never be
there the way I needed him to be, I was numb.

he just didn't care enough
and my heart was crushed

I wasn't his little girl anymore, I never was.
we would never have that father-daughter bond.

I learned sadness from my mother;
she said we only had each other.

she never let me speak,
I only hear her scream.

fear was the sound of her car
coming down the street.

what have I done to make her upset?
she hits me again, so I won’t forget.

she cries until I comfort her again,
while I choke on the smoke from her cigarette.

love shouldn't make you suffer;
she said we only had each other.

I learned sadness from my mother,
and I’m learning happiness,
without her.

it's hard when anger turns into empathy.
when you realize your mother and father
were once innocent, just like you.

they did not ask to be born, just like you.

just as their parents before them,
and their parents before them,
they were born without permission.

so, should I be angry at god?
who do I blame?

this anger is from my ancestors;
it lives in my veins.

my parents were born innocent;
something or someone made them change.

it was easier to be angry,
then it is to be filled with empathy.

I see myself in both of them;
my parents are my destiny.

I wish I could have loved my mother
enough to save her.

I wish she would have loved me enough
to save herself.

if I'm being honest,
I hope that sometime
before his death,
my father will realize
I am all he has left.

he will be heavy with regret,
and I will pretend to forget
all the things he did and didn't.

time will have softened his heart,
and made his body weak,
he will need me to care for him,
as I once needed him to care for me.

I still have hope
that he might change,
and I will wait for his love,
even if it comes late.

I wish I could have cried in my mother's arms,
but she was always crying in mine.

it was too heavy to carry as a child,
I didn't grow stronger, I grew tired.

I love her, I wanted to love all her sadness away.
but a child cannot heal their mother's pain.

seeing my parents through adult eyes

as the child within me dies

my father loves the pursuit of women,
more than anything

I used to think I was his everything

my mother is not as sure as she said she was

her opinion used to be the only one

I wasn't as defiant as they made me out to be

that was just an excuse for why they hurt me

just admit what you’ve done wrong,
tell me you understand that you’ve hurt me.
all I’ve ever wanted was your accountability.

I know you can’t change the past,
but the least you can do, without any excuse
is ask for my forgiveness.

why is it so hard to give me an apology?
all you do is deny, *I need your honesty*.

don’t say it didn’t happen,
or that we don’t remember it the same.
I am not a child anymore,
I won’t fall for your gaslighting.

weren't there any good times with your mom?

if I didn't complain and did everything she'd say
if I hid away and got good grades
if I accepted her rage and gave her space
if I didn't bother her with anything,
then it was okay.

trauma leads to trauma.
you don't know anything different,
than how you were raised.

when he slapped me
and said it was out of love,
I remember the same words
coming from my mom.

when he would leave me at night,
and I would cry all alone, I remember
my dad who never came home.

how can I love her
and hate her at the same time?

understand her and be disconnected
from her in the same thought?

I miss her, but I am relieved she is gone.
how do I let her go and still hold on?

I wanted to be a daddy's girl.
I wish he loved me more than anything in the world.

I wanted his love more than I wanted to be alive.
I wish he had made me part of his life.

I wanted to be his everything,
I wanted to stop him from leaving.

I wanted to be a daddy's girl,
I guess I'll keep on dreaming.

when people think of a trauma bond
they often think of romantic love,
but mine was with my mom.

the more she hurt me,
the more she tried to love me.

the more she tried to love me,
the more she realized she couldn't.

she couldn't love me the way
a mother should love their child.

she would love me like heaven
and then hurt me like hell.

healthy love didn't exist
between us, but I could never leave.

I was her daughter and she was my mom,
we loyally stayed in the never ending cycle
of a trauma bond.

my mother begged my father not to leave,
but he left anyway.

I’ve spent my life being what men want,
so I don’t have to beg them to stay.

I still have to beg,
and they leave anyway.

I respect my father's honesty,
he was unhappy with the life
he chose, so he chose differently,
(and he didn't choose me).

days with him turned into weekend visits,
weekend visits turned into monthly visits,
monthly visits turned into phone calls,
phone calls turned into texts.

now I barely speak to him at all.

I respect my father's honesty,
he was unhappy with the life
he chose, so he chose differently,
(and he didn't choose me).

but he is my father,
and I didn't have a choice.

I imagine my mother as a child.
at first, she is smiling as if the corners
of her lips are reaching for the sun.

then one day she notices her mother
crying while her father is drunk.
she doesn't know what's wrong,
she thought they were in love.

her dad eventually leaves
and her mom is mentally gone.
she always does her best but
her mother says she's wrong.

her mother screams:
"you are just like your father!
you have a big mouth just like him!"
that's when her light starts to fade,
and the darkness begins.

forgiving her and forgiving myself.
we held hands and walked through hell.
she loved me the only way she knew how,
I can't stay trapped in anger at my mother;
forgiveness is the only way out.

I can't keep blaming my parents,
it's time for me to change.

It doesn't matter what they did,
I must help myself anyway.

I never want my children
to feel the way I feel.

so now that I'm grown,
it is my responsibility to heal.

2.
dangerous love

toxic relationships and heartbreak

how did I end up here?
it’s a long, sad story,
beginning with a little girl
who was taught that love
was only given to others,
so she never learned to love herself.

he didn’t delicately hurt me
like a hollywood heartbreak.

he shattered the very essence of me.

I cared too much.
I would have peeled
flesh from my bones,
for the people I loved.

they expected my soul,
my body, and all the rest.
I gave all of me
until I had nothing left.

I thought I could escape myself
by being with someone else.

consuming them, mirroring them,
catering to their needs.

but every time they leave (and they always leave),
I am left just as before, unbearably empty.

the desire to be desired,
is a foolish wish.
I know that love
shouldn't hurt like this.

when he's not around,
I wonder who he's with.
but when he comes home,
I drink his poison with a kiss.

when you fall in love,
don't fall too far from yourself.

you shouldn't have to change everything
about you, to be with someone else.

there will be somebody who loves you
just as much as you love them.

love doesn't make you beg
and plead for attention.

my cashmere heart was broken apart,
with words that hurt like razor blades.

cutting deep inside my veins,
cherry blood with a metal taste.

time cannot fade these scars;
he destroyed me and made it look like art.

he was smiling as I fell apart,
I used to be the girl with a cashmere heart.

you cry and you scream
and you beg for the bare minimum.

but he won't comfort you as you need,
he won't come to you at all, he'll just leave.

why do you need to learn
the same lesson over again?

didn't your father already teach you that?

my submission turned into rebellion,
my kindness turned into aggression,
my forgiveness turned into revenge.

the abuse turned an innocent girl
into an angry woman.

love isn't always easy,
but it shouldn't feel like hell in your hands.

it shouldn't leave you empty,
desperate to understand.

love doesn't leave you wondering
what you've done wrong,

or threaten to leave,
if you're not getting along.

love doesn't force or demand,
or leave you alone for hours in the bed.

love isn't always easy,
but it shouldn't feel like hell in your hands.

when he’s angry, I wonder what I’ve done.
maybe it's that I’m not pretty enough.

when he’s angry I talk too much,
he pulls away quickly when I give him a hug.

when he’s angry, I wonder when he’ll leave.
I try so hard to fix everything.

when he’s angry, I just want to know why.
I ask him over and over; I beg and I cry.

when he’s angry, he says that he’s fine,
but then he goes to sleep, without saying goodnight.

all I ever felt on my skin
is hard hands that slap and hit.

I didn't know any other love than this.
tenderness was just a word that didn't seem to exist.

my mother would hit me
and then say she loved me more than anything.

I learned that love wasn't love without pain.

that's why I believed he loved me,
as he destroyed me again and again.

I want to know why I am expected to forgive
people who don't want to be forgiven.

who have ripped me apart from the inside out
and then told me to stop being a victim.

I want to know why I am told to forget it
because everybody makes mistakes.

while they get to move on with their lives,
I get to live in constant heartbreak.

I want to know why the anger of the abused
is less important than forgiving the abuser.

why do they deserve forgiveness
when they damaged me in ways I never deserved?

I want to know why the world cares more about
forgiveness, than the pain of those who were hurt.

holding my breath so that he can breathe,
I am only worthy when I agree.

my submission is his freedom;
I am only beautiful without an opinion.

he's not sure if I'm the one,
if I disagree, he says he's done.

becoming what he wants,
so he won't leave.

staying silent
by clenching my teeth.

holding my breath so that he can breathe,
I am only worthy when I agree.

I let him hurt me
just so he would feel me,
and maybe be the one to heal me.

but he didn’t even care
that he caused me pain.

I wanted to be someone to him,
even if I was the one he would break.

my friends ask me why I don't leave.

he says I'm crazy…
that I am not remembering things right,
I pushed him first; I started the fight.

at first, the bruises were pink.
I like the colour pink; it reminds me of love.
he must love me.

now they've gone blue and green.
he says I am beautiful when I bleed;
I've become a corpse of me.

"why don't you just leave?"

I remember a time when I thought he would change,
when I thought my love would take his anger away.

I would be so soft and do whatever he'd say,
run myself into the ground with a smile on my face.

if I could grin and bear it, even for one more day,
maybe he would feel my love and he would change.

he didn't care about my love;
he just wanted me to obey.

I sacrificed myself for a man
who could never be saved.

he said I was dangerous and called me a witch.
I wonder how many innocent women
have been burned alive because of men like him.

my bathwater has gone cold,
but it keeps me warmer,
and holds me closer
than your neglectful hands.

I've been lying here so long,
waiting for you to come home,
my bathwater has gone cold.

a wolf will still devour you when he's hungry,
no matter how much you've loved him.

I guess I held on because hope never dies;
it never dies until death.

I didn't realize that hope doesn't work with the devil,
and that he wants you to keep believing he will change.

hope is his weapon,
hope is his knife against your throat
while he tells you how much he loves you.

hope is his hands getting tighter around your neck,
hope is his smile as he watches you struggle
to take a breath.

the only kind of hope that exists with him,
is the hope of death.

(he will end up killing you if you don't leave him)

he killed the warmth of the sun,
green turned to grey.
if roses were my dreams,
they've all wilted away.

to the girl who makes excuses for his excuses
and embraces cold sheets in an empty bed,
to the girl who wonders when he will
come home or answer the text.

to the girl who tries to find hope,
where hope has never been,
I once was the girl who didn't believe,
she was worthy of basic human decency.

but we are worth so much more than the basic,
and we will be just fine on our own.
we will no longer hold on to men
who don't serve us.

it's time to let them go.

he said he adored me.
now he is bored of me.

he said he loved my faith,
but I couldn't keep him faithful.

I look at his eyes;
he is looking away.

I promised I wouldn't get attached;
he promised he would stay.

but we are both liars, anyway.

maybe he will come over
and tell me to come to bed.

(he won't)

maybe he will hold my hand
and ask me to forget.

(he won't)

maybe he will apologize
for all the cruel things he said.

(he won't)

maybe he will treat me
like he did when we first met.

(he won't)

he only loves me when I'm happy,
when I make him feel like a man,

smiling cheek to cheek,
giving all that I am.

but when I break into pieces,
smaller than sand,

he lets me slip through his fingers,
and I'm alone again.

be very careful with a delicate woman.
if she breaks, the parts of her you left so unloved
will cut through you like slivers of glass:
too small to remove but too sharp to forget.

I knew the difference between love and lust
when I shattered to the floor like a broken plate
and he stepped right over me to get away.

when I was no longer pretty,
my eyes running black with tears and hate,
he didn't even bring me a cloth to wipe my face.

I explained to him my heart,
but he didn't understand.
the sadness understood me more than him.

he couldn't wait to leave me,
he said I was “too much.”
I wasn't worthy of his love unless I let him touch.

women fall in love with their ears,
men fall in love with their eyes.

he watches me become a fool,
believing all his lies.

he tells me that he loves me,
but can't give me the reasons why.

he falls asleep beside me,
as I lay awake and cry.

I beg him to change,
but he won't even try.

women fall in love with their ears,
men fall in love with their eyes.

I put all my happiness into a man,
he promised me forever
and I believed him.

then I had to start asking him to look at me
instead of his phone. he would say nothing
was wrong and then leave me alone.

call after call went to voicemail,
hours after he said he'd be home,
falling asleep and waking up on my own.

I remember the way his hands held me so tightly,
I remember how they let me go.

you will never be good enough for him,
there will always be something to criticize.

when you tell him what he's done to you,
he will say you're spreading lies.

what's the point in trying?
he'll never love you the way he should.

you keep making excuses for his behaviour,
but *if he wanted to, he would.*

when I decide I'm done, I'll already be gone.
the sound of me leaving will echo like a song.

I've been the type of woman who keeps holding
on, even when my hands are bleeding,
telling me it's wrong.

my higher self won't let me stay where I don't belong.
when you feel me let go of you, I'll already be gone.

leaving is hard,
but it's harder to stay.

he keeps showing you who he is,
but you turn the other way.

you still have hope,
but he's not going to change.

starting over is scary,
but you have to be brave.

I say I wish I'd never met him, but what I mean is…

I wish I had loved myself enough to be alone,
I wish he'd been a kinder soul,
I wish I didn't spend my nights waiting by the phone.

I wish that he had loved me,
(the way he loved to be cruel).
I wish I'd been a wiser girl,
and known more about the world.

I wish I hadn't wasted my younger years,
I wish I'd laughed more and not drowned in tears,
I wish I'd left him sooner despite my fears.

I wish I'd known my worth,
and he hadn't been my first.
I wish my heart wasn't broken and burned,
I wish I didn't live with his curse.

I wish I'd never met him…

she never came back,
the girl I was before he broke me.

I waited and waited,
I hoped, and I prayed.

her light left one evening,
and the darkness stayed.

there is only one thing
more dangerous than an abusive man:

the women who stand behind him,
even when they know what he's done.

a poem for my ex:

everyday is the same with you,
your cruelty is predictable.

there is nothing special about you,
except for your psychopathy.
(even narcissists are common these days)

you are a horrible lover,
I faked it every time.

so far life has taught you
that you can get away with anything.

so when I left, you waged war,
but I had already won.
leaving you was my greatest victory.

if I see you in another life, I'll turn the other way.
I'll make good friends, read books in the sun,
I won't even breathe in your direction.

if I see you in another life, you won't make me cry.
I'll hold my head up and I'll walk by.

in another life, you'll be less than a stranger.
I won't have all the pain;
and I'll be the girl I should have been.

If I see you in another life…

you spit me out, but you can't get
my taste out of your mouth.
the agony of losing me tortures your tongue.

at the end of your life when you think of the
people you love and all your regrets,

it will always be me and the day that we met.

you know what you've done,
but to say it out loud
is too brutal a reality.
it would be suicide by honesty,
and you are such a coward.

I remember lying on the kitchen floor
wondering if I'd ever get up again.

wondering if it was even worth getting up,
because every time I did,
he kicked me harder to the floor.

I was so numb that even with his hands
around my neck, part of me didn't care.
I'd been afraid of death for so long, that I lost the fear.

I submitted to his cruelty, it was all that I'd known,
and somehow the abuse felt safer than being alone.
he broke all of me until I fell apart.

eventually, I got away, but I'll never be the same.
part of me will always be the girl on the kitchen
floor, wondering if I'll get up again.

when they say, "but you survived!"
I smile and nod.

I look around and look within,
for any sign of life or remnants of who I had been.

she’s gone (the girl I used to be).
my heart was destroyed, I survived only physically.

I can’t remember a day I haven't cried;
is this what it means to be alive?

they watch me barely holding onto life,
and then they say, "but you survived!”

I am a woman of god,
full of poems and sin.
my sensuality is a blessing,
abused by men.

I thought I found my true love after heartbreak,
but you were just a test to see if I learned anything.

you were there as a reminder not to trust men
who say they love me but don't act like they do.

I thought you had my back,
but you stood behind me and stabbed me in it.

everything about us was a lie,
now I am the fool who is heartbroken twice.

he looked at her in black and white,
she wanted to be seen in colour.

it felt good to act like nothing ever happened,
like it wasn't the beginning of our end.

to act like we were still lovers,
and we were still friends.

before all the lying and the fights,
I wanted to pretend, if only for one night.

please stop talking to me
as if we're acquaintances.

you know the insides of me,
the warm and tortured insides of me,

all of which you promised to love,
all of which you left behind.

I prefer silence to the sadness
of being misunderstood.

it doesn’t matter how I explain my heart,
he doesn’t love me the way he should.

days go by without words,
and he doesn’t ask what’s wrong
like I thought he would.

but I still prefer silence to the sadness
of being misunderstood.

crying alone,
eight hours looking at my phone,
no sleep and no reply from you.

the idea that you could love me
was just that: *an idea*.

reality hits hard when you know
how the story ends.

you lost me that night
while I stayed awake,
distressed for a text.

I am not the same girl
who waits around
and hopes for the best.

no one talks about the heartbreak
that comes when two people love
each other deeply but know it's not right.

a mutual understanding,
a mutual goodbye.
no anger, no hate, no fights.

wishing it was different,
and knowing that it's not.
when love just isn't enough,
but you both wish it was.

I obsess about small things,
like the paper cut on my finger
or the bruise on my leg,
which I keep pushing on, so I feel the pain.

I obsess about small things
that you said or you didn't
(but I wish you would),
which I can't stop thinking about
(though I wish I could).

I will not be the person you settle for,
because you haven't found someone else.

I deserve a love that chooses me, again and again.
even with a thousand women standing before him.

I am not your trial run love,
or the in-between to keep you warm.

while you are waiting for her,
I will not be the person you settle for.

if you touched my soul
the way you touched my body,
I would be the happiest woman in the world.

but your hands do most of the talking,
and when I'm not in the mood
there isn't much to say.

I wrote this for us,
or what we could have been

in another time or dimension,
before our love was crushed
by the weight of this world.

I would have rubbed your back until you fell asleep,
and watched every minute of your favourite movie.

you would have made me laugh until it hurt,
and let me sleep in your favourite t-shirt.

our love was too beautiful to be seen,
so I wrote this for us, or what we could have been.

I have an ache in my bones
for someone to love, someone to hold.
it's just so hard because my mind knows,
my heart is so much better being left alone.

are we really in love
or are we just too afraid to be unloved?

if you only knew how quickly I'd answer your call,
how I'd run into your arms and forget it all.

if you said, “let's try it again.”
I would try until the very end.

but I know you won't call,
you don't feel the way I feel.

loving you and losing you,
is the wound that never heals.

I don't think about you anymore, except when
I'm leaving for work, I can't find my keys,
and I remember your sweet smile,
as you would hand them to me.

I don't think about you anymore,
unless I'm in the shampoo aisle and I think of the time
I got mad at you for using mine; you told me it was
because you wanted to smell like me,
so it was like I was with you all the time.

I don't think about you anymore,
aside from the evening when the sun
shines perfectly on your side of the bed,
and I realize you'll never lay there with me again.

I don't think about you anymore,
but then I hear that song,
you spun me around and around
like we were in a stupid rom-com.

I don't think about you anymore,
apart from being awake,
or asleep, or anywhere in between.

the memory of you is the death that keeps killing me.

if we get another chance,
I promise to make things right.

every morning I will greet you with
a kiss, I'll never go to sleep angry again.

nothing but kind words will be spoken,
and our home will be a home where
hearts aren't broken.

we will undo all the wrongs,
the little things won't cause a fight.

I know I'll make mistakes
but I won't make them twice.

if we get another chance,
I promise to make things right.

if we meet again in this life or the next,
please know that every second we've been apart,
my lips have never grown tired of saying your name
and my heart has never stopped aching for your love.

life felt so hopeful,
your smile made everything okay,
(just your smile).

I finally felt safe for the first time in my life
and it was strange how I changed
when I wasn't afraid.

you kissed my cheeks when you thought I was asleep,
when life felt like hell, you were my peace.

life is full of love and loss,
there is always someone new.

I will go on and pretend I am okay,
but there will never be another you.

I hope you are happy now,
even though it's not with me.

I hope someone is waiting
for you at home with a smile.

I hope you wake up each day
excited to see them.

I hope you understand
each other effortlessly.

I hope you remember me,
the way I remember you.

I hope you are happy now,
I wish I was too.

"pack your bags and get out!"

"but you are all I have
and there is nowhere to go.
you are here, you are my home."

(I'm sorry)

my atoms are angry;
I am sick of being half-loved,
with complex conditions,
compared to greater minds,
and tighter bodies.

I want your soul to see mine and say,
"this way, this way. no matter what happens
I am here with you. let's go this way."

you can't make someone love you
by loving them harder.

every time I moved closer,
you would go farther.

I wanted to remember,
but you deleted the picture.

in the end, we had very little love left,
not even a whisper.

3.
invisible wounds

depression and mental health

what doesn't kill you makes you:

lose your innocence-
not trust anyone ever again-
wonder what makes you so unlovable-
live your life in a constant state of survival-
question everything you thought you knew-
think about all the ways it could have been different-
ask yourself if it's worth going on with all the pain-
wake up each morning and contemplate the same.

what doesn’t kill you
kills parts of yourself
you will never get back.

it is easier to have conversations with the devil,
than it is to listen to myself.

even the devil has been kinder to me,
then the voice inside my head.

and I guess that's why the evil keeps winning,
over and over again

give me back my girlhood,
the world stole it from me.
I want the gift I was promised but never received.

erase the memories and everything I know,
I want to be ignorant and believe there are
diamonds in the snow.

let me be a child and a daydreamer,
not an adult and a failure.

I want to have hope, I want to believe,
I want the gift I was promised but never received.

I'm only connected to the disconnection.
everything is impermanent,
and nothing makes me feel anymore.

except for my sadness,
which constantly reminds me
that I am still warm inside.

I am bleeding from invisible wounds,
as hot tears burn streaks down my pale cheeks,
and I never stop thinking about you.

I am allowed to grieve who I used to be.

the little girl with so many dreams,
eyes that saw a kind world
with endless possibilities.

an unbroken heart that didn't hurt to beat,
a smile that could find happiness in anything.

I didn't deserve what happened to me,
and I am allowed to grieve who I used to be.

they called me beautiful like it was my name.

it was the identity they gave me,
an expectation I could never live up to.

they told me to smile and talk more softly,
so, I screamed and I screamed.

rage killed my beauty.
nobody loves an angry girl.

right now, I just want to feel okay,
even if nothing is okay.

I've already felt the pain,
so how long do I have to keep feeling it
before it goes away?

I don't feel at home in myself.
every day I wake up confused.

I am a stranger wandering the streets of my mind,
lost with no direction, desperate to be accepted.

searching for any part of myself I recognize,
trying to find my way home.

no matter where I am or who I am with,
without myself, *I am alone.*

death looks at me with sympathy
as I struggle to stay alive.

it tempts me in my misery,
making it seem easier to die.

my heart starts to race, it jumps into my throat,
I swallow it back down and I try not to choke.

I hold my heart and I try to breathe,
with every breath there is hope.

death looks at me with sympathy,
but it's not my time to go.

sitting in my car crying,
I have nowhere else to go.
even when I am home,
I don't feel at home.

I wonder if someone will see me
and ask if I'm okay.
it would feel good to be seen,
although I'd feel ashamed.

I wanted more than this.
I can't believe I ended up like this.

why does being alive feel like I'm dying?

I say I'm going for a drive,
but I'm sitting in my car crying.

down
down
down
she goes.

into that endless black hole.
no ladder, no hand of a friend,
nothing can make the darkness end.

the way I found God,
is the same way I lost him.

head down, on my knees,
devoting myself and ready to bleed.

I was crying so hard,
grinding my teeth,

desperate to taste the mercy and relief
they promise you will have

if you only believe.

a soft death,
the kind that comes while you're still alive,
without you even noticing,
slowly from the inside.

hope begins to feel a little less hopeful,
the sky looks grey.
they tell me that I’m beautiful,
but I don't feel that way.

life leaves the party quietly,
now there is nothing left.
nobody even notices that I am dying
a soft death.

when people tell me to stop crying
and not to be weak, I revolt in tears.

may they drown in my sadness.
let them feel the strength in my misery.

if I don't wake, let me dream,
let me rot beneath the sheets.

don't tell me that the day awaits;
the sun burns my eyes anyway.

if I don't wake, leave me in peace,
and let me rot beneath the sheets.

every day I wake up and I hope
something will change,
but all I see are more lines on my face.

time passes by, there is only decay.
all my prayers keep running away.

the darkness is afraid of my depression,
there is no escape, but every day I wake up
and I hope something will change.

you said you wanted all of me, so here I am.
darkness, melancholy, rage.
why are you walking away?

a cage in search of a bird,
or anything that will fill the void
that lives inside of me.

even a hand to hold through cold metal bars
is hope enough that something beautiful exists
outside of this prison.

(my mind)

I rotted away slowly,
like an apple in the fridge.

its decay is inevitable,
no matter how its life is prolonged.

as is my sadness,
no matter how much I pretend to be happy.

I've survived and I am not stronger for it.

I am not proud to wear the scars,
they are a reminder of the pain I've endured.
although my body has healed,
my mind still bleeds like they are fresh.

people around me have become so tired of the
same story and I don't even tell it anymore.
I wish they understood that I'm tired too.
tired of pretending that I'm okay,
and that "time heals all wounds" (it doesn't)

the trauma literally changed my brain.
overstimulated amygdala,
underactive hippocampus,
weak prefrontal cortex.

I've survived and I am not stronger for it.

I am a waste of a lovely face,
my lips are always red with rage.

crying in an empty bathtub,
using my tears to fill it up.

I'm sad again, I'm remembering,
I'm obsessing, I'm ruminating.

I can't stop thinking,
my heart keeps breaking.

nothing makes it go away,
I am a waste of a lovely face.

nobody can love me,
(that's what he would say)

4.
no more tomorrow

death and grief

I've made peace with grief.

I let it kiss me on the cheek
and tuck me into bed.
I know it will greet me
when I wake up again.

grief holds my hand
as I walk down the street.
I taste it on my tongue
with everything I eat.

I don't fight it anymore,
grief always wins the war.
it fills me up when I feel hollow,
and reminds me that one day,
there will be no tomorrow.

(and I will get to see you again)

this time last year, you were still alive.

I'm looking out onto the road, remembering
the cars going by as we'd speak on the phone.

now I watch them go by all alone,
I wish your voice was still on the line.

how can everything be just as it was and
completely different at the same time?

how can everyone just go on with life?

I miss the sound of your voice and listening to you
complain. I miss everything about you, I used to hate.

maybe forever is the
acceptance of impermanence.

when the mind tells the eyes,
this could be the last time,
every second becomes a treasure.

maybe forever isn't all of time.
maybe forever is in this very moment, with you.

my grandmother and I stood
over my mother's body.

we guarded it as if her death
was an approaching army.

teary-eyed, we stared at each other with grief,
desperate for her to stay, but desperate for her relief.

we pretended to be strong, we talked about god,
and all the things in life we'd done wrong.

my grandmother and I stood
over my mother's body.

she stroked her daughter's hair;
I caressed my mother's arm.

we acted prepared to lose her,
but we weren't ready to move on.

my mother was so much more than her ending;
she was a woman, a daughter, a mother, a soul.

my grandmother and I stood
over my mother's body, trying to let her go.

my mother is dying.
I listen to silent regret fall from her eyes
onto hollow cheeks.

her dry lips move, as she whispers to speak.

“I don't feel like I will die,” she cries.
“none of us make it out alive,” I cry.
“I wish we had more time,” she cries.
“*I wish we had all of time*,” I cry.

she died before we could fix things,
before we could make things right.

I would give anything to hug her again,
or even have one last fight.

she said things would get better,
but it didn't work out that way.

we had so much to work through
and now it's too late.

I am left with so many unsettled feelings,
she died before we could fix things.

maybe in heaven,
she will understand the weight
of her anger on my chest.
she will lift me, twirl me around,
and I will breathe again.

maybe in heaven,
I won't have to explain how she hurt me;
she will apologize without denial,
and *I will forgive her again.*

maybe in heaven,
her sadness will be happiness instead.
we will have another chance
because god will make us forget.

maybe in heaven,
with no words left unsaid,
she will be the mother that I needed,
and we will try again.

(maybe in heaven)

.

she is gone,
I am still here,
and everything feels different now.

I am torn between "nothing matters,"
and "absolutely everything does,"
floating in the space between both possibilities,

I am numb,
I am lost,
I am different.

everything feels different now.

on the way home from work,
I want to call you and tell you about my day.

I've been so lost without you and
I can't believe it ended this way.

I still read the texts you sent me
promising it would be okay,

but the night is still dark,
and I am still afraid.

I wish that it was different,
or that you'd stayed the same.

the anger was forgotten;
now only love remains.

on the way home from work,
I want to call you and tell you about my day.

she watched me take my first breath;
I watched her take her last.

life felt like it dragged on slowly,
but then it went by so fast.

she didn't want to hurt me;
I didn't want to hurt her.

our love was like fire,
and we both got burned.

I forgive her for what she did,
and I hope she forgives me.

the love that's left between us
is now only my grief.

I asked her to hold on one more day.
her silence answered, "I can't."

she watched me take my first breath;
I watched her take her last.

I try and describe my grief,
but my grief is everything.

it's the uneasy feeling that lingers after a bad dream,
shadows on the wall that seem to come from nothing.

the smell of cigarettes and an unworn dress,
her empty room with her empty bed.

realizing how much we suffered the same,
starting to accept that I'll never see her again.

I try to describe my grief, I want to give it a name,
but my grief is infinite, *my grief is everything*.

I wonder if she looks down on me in heaven,
with disappointment in her eyes.

maybe death has helped her see,
how hard I tried.

I did everything I could,
to be a good daughter and friend.

the truth poured out of me in poems,
I couldn't hold it in.

I kept all our secrets until she died,
but I couldn't keep on living with all the lies.

I wonder if she looks down on me in heaven,
with disappointment in her eyes.

grief sits like a lump on my chest,
suffocating me. grief is my new friend;
it sits at the table with my anxiety.

grief is being at the grocery store
and hearing her favourite song.

grief is one of those days,
where everything keeps going wrong.

grief is being so angry and lonely
and hopeless at the same time.

grief is continuing to live like everything is fine.

they tell me to get over it.
"it was just a dog!"
but she was *my* dog.

when humans hurt me,
she loved me, loyally.

her brown fur turned to grey,
and her eyes clouded like a rainy day,
but she loved me until she slept, indefinitely.

I miss the sound of her paws on the floor,
and the way she always waited for me by the door.

she wasn't just a dog,
she was my dog;
she was my everything.

that split second when you wake up,
you haven't realized it yet
and everything is okay.

then the dread of remembering
hits you like a nightmare in daylight.

they are gone forever,
you are still alive
and nothing feels right.

I think of the last time.

the last time we had coffee
the last time we went for a walk
the last time we sat together
the last time we had a good talk
the last time we watched our favourite show
the last time we laughed until we cried
the last time a small thing turned into a fight
the last time I told you I love you
the last time you walked out the door

I didn't know it was the last time,
now I understand why every moment is precious.

everything feels ordinary until it is a memory.

until we meet again,
I will wake up every day and I will try.

try to move on without you,
in whatever ways I can,
one foot in front of the other,
over and over again.

you told me to remember to breathe,
so I am breathing. hurting and healing,
with the rise and fall of my breath.

your absence has changed everything;
without you I am afraid.
you told me that all will be well,
so I am being brave.

I haven't made it through one day
where the thought of you doesn't make me cry.

until we meet again,
I will wake up every day
and I will try.

I can't talk to you anymore,
so I talk to the moon and the stars.

I ask them to carry my words,
to wherever you are.

when the funeral is over,
and the condolences no longer come,

people start asking about your day,
instead of how you're holding up.

the initial shock begins to wear off,
but nothing is the same and you feel lost.

that's when the real grieving begins,
when it is quiet, and everyone has moved on,

when the funeral is over
and the condolences no longer come.

I should have held you tighter
and not let go.

(I thought I'd get another hug)

I should have told you all the ways
I love you, one last time.

(I thought I'd tell you later)

I shouldn't have assumed
I would get another chance.

(I thought I would see you again)

when the world forgets,
I will remember.

I will remember the warmth of your hands
even after they've gone cold,

the sound of your voice,
even after it's gone quiet.

(it's so quiet without you.)

I will remember the way you cried
even when I can't see your eyes,

the way you took your last breath
as if you were relieved to meet death.

I will remember the life you lived,
and mourn the life you didn't get.

no matter how much time goes by,
with every sunrise and sunset,

I will remember,
even when the world forgets.

I hope that death feels like my mother calling me
home from the kitchen window, while I'm playing
outside with my friends.

it's a soft summer evening and I'm tired from
riding my bike. she's made my favourite meal
and everything's alright.

she asks about my day as we eat and I tell her
everything, as if this one day is all that's ever been.

she runs me a bath and washes my hair,
she lets me splash the water everywhere.

she wraps me in a towel and kisses me on the cheek,
the love she gives is all I need.

I put on my pajamas and get into bed,
I feel so clean, comfortable and fresh.

she reads my favourite story again and again,
and as my eyes start to close, I hear her whisper:

"the end."

though she hurt me so much on earth,
when they ask me who I want to see in heaven,
it will always be her.

5.
the renewal

love and healing

healing is the hardest part.

I force my eyes open
after my alarm has been going off
for over an hour and I am already late.

I hate the light; I hate the heat
and the cold and the night.
my feet hit the floor and they feel heavy.

I just want to sleep but I don't want to dream;
I can't manage everything,
so I slow down and breathe.

I'm nowhere near who I thought I'd be.
why is everyone else so happy? what about me?

they say it comes slowly,
but I have no idea where to start.

healing is the hardest part.

mothering the child within,
comforting myself,
the way I never received from anyone else.

crossing my arms around my body,
embracing the little girl who needs a hug.
together we will get through this,
we were always enough.

here, only with me,
she doesn't need to swallow down the sadness,
her emotions are safe to be free.

the little girl inside,
kept waiting for someone to save her,
she never imagined,
she would be her own saviour.

without light we can't see the shadows,
without love we can't feel the pain.

isn't it beautiful to find out
that we are not alone
in our suffering?

after years of feeling as if no one
could understand our torment,
we are found together,
sitting gently with our sorrow.

knowing that you have felt it and survived,
makes the pain a bit easier to take.

the day will still come,
no matter how hard you close your eyes.

the night will still kiss the day goodbye,
painting colours in the sky.

welcome the darkness. embrace the light.
don't fight against the ups and downs of life.

sometimes the sun shines, even when it rains.
so I try to find goodness, despite all the pain.

I found pieces of myself
after losing them in misery.

if you're wondering
if you'll ever find yourself again,
you will, but it will come *after the breaking*.

when life piles up the pain on your chest
and you can barely take a breath.

after you've shattered to the floor from all the pain,
and all you can do is sweep up the pieces
and throw them away.

you will find yourself after you let go,
and stop thinking, and healing,
and searching for that feeling.

when you accept that beautiful things are broken,
and the pieces you are looking for,
are found in this moment.

I suffered, I learned, I changed.
I became myself again.

I let go of who I thought I was,
and embraced who I became.

I suffered, I learned, I changed.
I became myself again.

it feels wrong.
so, it is.

there is no need to argue with the voice within;
you can ignore it for a while,
but then it will make you listen.

it feels wrong.
so, it is.

staring out the window,
dust floating in sunbeams,
it's then that I realize

there is not one single impossibility.

the air holds the dirt so delicately,
it is so free inside the light.
maybe if I keep floating,
I can make it through this life.

the forest does not resist the blaze.
the trees stand tall despite the flames,
and I will not fall despite the pain.

relief will come as tears fall like rain.
the fire will go out,
and the forest will be born again.

(and so will you)

I have searched for love in people, places and things.
I have begged for love crying on my knees.

I have wished for love like the stars could hear me,
I have thought about love for hours trying to find its
meaning

I have looked for it everywhere, wondering if it even
exists. I have mistaken love for a player’s kiss.

I have searched for love all over and in everybody else.
when I couldn't find it anywhere,
I learned to love myself.

what they don't tell you about trauma healing:

- trauma doesn't just go away,
  some of it always stays.
- you'll never be the same, part of you,
  (maybe all of you) will be forever changed.
- life feels different and the pain is infinite.
- it affects every choice and relationship.
- you'll lose friends, they won't be able to
  understand your darkness.
- healing will go on for a long time,
  probably for the rest of your life.
- you won't feel better until you physically/
  emotionally/mentally feel it and stop being
  afraid to let it exist.
- you must stop chasing who you were
  before and allow a new version to be born.
- you'll be angry and you'll mourn who
  you used to be.
- once you feel the grief, you'll begin healing.

he was the love
that made me believe in love again.

they say home is a place,
but a home without your love
is just walls and a bed.

when I lay with you, head on your chest,
I seek refuge from the storm.

there in your arms, I find pieces of myself,
and you return them with peace.

they say home is a place,
but you are home to me.

see me without eyes, kiss me without lips.
walk inside my thoughts and listen.

touch me entirely without using your hands,
you don't need to feel me to understand.

I am more than my body, hair and face.
I want to feel our souls embrace.

he made me laugh.
he helped me escape
the pain of my thoughts,
if only for a moment.

he made me laugh,
it's how he loved me.

you make me feel like I belong,
like I don't need to be 'someone.'
I can just be me and that is enough.

I never felt a love that didn't demand to receive.
you give and you give and don't ask for anything
in my happiness and my grief,
you allow me to just be.

you tell me everything I do right
after I confess all I've done wrong.
without expectations and nothing in return,
you make me feel like I belong.

I want to lay with you on a pillow of stars,
floating forever, like the galaxy is ours.

I want the kind of love
that loves me when I'm too much.

the kind of love that lets me be,
and knows I am enough.

the kind of love that accepts me,
even as I change.

the kind of love that I can ride,
despite all the waves.

the kind of love that can see me smile
and know I'm not okay.

the kind of love that holds me down
but always lets me grow.

the kind of love that sees my rage
and loves me even more.

other girls dreamed of being somebody,
I dreamed of being loved by somebody.

love me as the sun
loves the land and sea.
I'm dirt and tears
and need all the warmth
you can give to me.

everybody wants to be something
in this world, and I guess I do, too.

but all I want, at the end of it all,
is to mean something to you.

I cannot remember a time when I didn't love you.
even before we met, I loved you.

you were always in my heart
as a thought, a hope, a dream.

my love for you has always been.

there is simplicity in loving you,
it comes without thought or effort.

it is the easiest thing I have ever done,
instinctually I knew you were the one.

I get goosebumps all over my mind
when I remember the night
your eyes made love with mine.

you turned me inside out,
undressing me with your soul,
layer by layer, down to the bone.

your mouth is a halo
and every time you speak,
your words breathe light into me.

what is love, except compromise and consideration?
to meet each other halfway and reflect on how each
decision will affect the other.

I melt into you.
heart to heart,
eye to eye,
hand to throat.

he held her like the universe holds the stars,
all her beauty and all her scars
in the palms of his hands, like a prayer to god.

he held her like the universe holds the stars.
he whispers, "I'll be with you wherever you are."

even when hope faded from close to far,
he held her like the universe holds the stars.

I've heard you can't love again until you've healed.
so, when he is tending to my wounds,
what is this warmth that I feel?

magic lives on his lips.
I crawl on my hands and knees
to taste his kiss.

I've never felt so beautiful.
the sky is no longer blue.
whenever I look up, all I see is you.

whatever light does to darkness,
you do to my heart.

soft hands
move slow,
across places
I never knew existed,
in my own mind,
on my own body.

when death greets me, and the earth absorbs me;
when my body becomes nutrients for the soil
and everything I am dissolves into nothingness.
when our memory becomes black
in the silence of the dirt, I will love you.

I will love you in the absence of existence,
I will love you when my life is so far gone,
even god forgets that I was created.

my love for you is immortal,
it is the only thing I get to keep.
when life as we know it is gone,
my love for you will be eternal energy.

the way the moon only glows because of the sun,
my heart only beats because of your love.

love has softened me and moulded me like clay.
I have hit rock bottom so many times,
but now when I fall I don't break.

you catch me

you are the only one who knows
my silence means I have so much to say.
you listen to me when I don't say a word.

your eyes have hands of their own;
every glance is an embrace.
I love the way you stare at me,
don't look away.

(eye contact)

I was searching for the perfect one,
but your imperfections
were what made me fall in love.

kiss me where it hurts,
(it hurts everywhere).

kiss me until the pain goes away,
(there are not enough hours in the day).

all your body and all your hair,
the space between my fingers,
I need you there.

as I was falling in love with him,
he made me fall in love with myself.

he loved me,

right then and there,
before we were anything,
and he owed me nothing.

bare bones and ashes of myself,
eyes with pits blacker than hell,

he loved me.

when I was least myself,
when I lost myself,
burned in the fire trying to find myself,

he loved me.

they say that love is blind,
but I don't think that's true.

I see all that you are
(the good and the bad)
and I still choose to love you.

6.
nurturing

motherhood

and just like that,

he fell from heaven
into all the chaos,
and called me, "mother."

you were the first heart
that lived inside of me,
other than my own.

what an honour it was,
to have your love
growing within me.

for the mothers who saw darkness
instead of light and didn't know why.
who felt as if their own child was foreign
in their arms, no matter how hard they tried.

for the mothers who felt dread in the morning
and at night, who struggled every second of the
day fighting with their mind.

for the mothers who didn't feel like they were good
enough to be mothers and wished they didn't exist.
who wanted to disappear but somehow found the
strength to resist.

for the mothers who went to hell and back with every
breath, while the world told them that being a mom was
the best. who felt like a ghost holding a baby, completely
unknown. crawling through the blackness all alone.

(you are not alone)

I look at my body, my womb, and my soul,
and I ask God, why did you let these children grow?

why did you let their souls pass through time,
from peace and perfection, into a life like mine?

my mind is corrupt, and my heart is all broken;
their cries for my love are so perfectly spoken.

how can I love them the way they deserve,
when I never felt loved, so love was never learned?

I want to be the mother I never had,
the mother that they deserve.

protect them, love them,
and hold their hearts
like glass in my hands.

in many ways,
I am no different than my children,
looking around, desperate for comfort.

in many ways,
I am just like my mother.
left alone to bear it all with no idea how.

I don’t try to do it all anymore,
I let love lead instead.

I want to be the mother that they deserve,
the mother I never had.

he travelled through my body
from a place much better than this.

he held me as I held him,
and gave me a reason to live.

time, be still.

let me live forever
in this moment with them.

I never knew the true loves
of my life, would be my children.

I pour my love into them,
they will never be thirsty.

they will never have to drink from an empty cup,
searching for someone to fill it up.

they will never feel like a burden,
to the one who should treat them like a treasure.

I kiss the backs of their hands,
loving them is such an honour.

they come before anything else or any other,
it is a privilege to be their mother.

there is no greater love
than that between a mother and child.

it's the only love that loves unconditionally,
the only love I know for certain will never go away.

I never understood true love before my children,
I don't think I've ever truly loved before them.

there aren't enough words to express my love,
nor enough time to show my love.

even the word love isn't enough,
it is an insult to this feeling, to call it love.

it is all-encompassing, it is infinite,
it is my beginning and my end.

I would do anything for their happiness,
their smile is my smile.

there is no greater love
than that between a mother and child.

if I had only one wish, it would be
that I am worthy enough for my children.

that despite all my mistakes, they will
always feel loved and safe.

they will look back on me fondly,
my memory will be a source of love and peace.

if I had only one wish, it would be
that my children never have to heal from me.

some days I suffer more than I survive
but my storm will never get them wet.

when I don't have the strength,
I will pretend.

I'll lock the door and cry in the shower,
my children won't worry about their mother.

they will feel secure, they will get to be kids.
they won't spend their childhood distressed like I did.

acknowledgements:

thank you to m and my children for loving and supporting me no matter what. thank you to my fellow poets and writers who have continuously encouraged me to write the book and finish the book. finally, *to my readers, who have given my voice the freedom to be heard. none of this would be possible without you.*

connect on all social media platforms > @rosebrikpoet